THE FRAGRANCE OF JESUS

Glimpsing the Kingdom through His Miracles

PATRICK COGHLAN

THE FRAGRANCE OF JESUS

Copyright © 2009 Patrick Coghlan
Original edition published in English under the title THE FRAGRANCE OF JESUS by Kevin Mayhew Ltd, Buxhall, England.
This edition copyright © Fortress Press 2019

All rights reserved. Except for brief quotations in critical articles or reviews, no part of this book may be reproduced in any manner without prior written permission from the publisher. Email copyright@augsburgfortress.org or write to Permissions, Fortress Press, PO Box 1209, Minneapolis, MN 55440-1209.

Scripture quotations taken from the Holy Bible, New International Version. Copyright © 1973, 1978, 1984 by International Bible Society. Used by permission of Hodder & Stoughton. A division of Hodder Headline Ltd. All rights reserved.

Cover image: Photo by Pepe Reyes on unsplash
Cover design: Joe Reinke

Print ISBN: 978-1-5064-5964-6

But thanks be to God, who always leads us
in triumphal procession in Christ and through
us spreads everywhere the fragrance of
the knowledge of him. For we are to God
the aroma of Christ among those who
are being saved and those who are perishing.

2 Corinthians 2:14–15.

Contents

About the Author	7
Introduction	9
1. Freedom Matthew 8:1–4 A man with leprosy	11
2. The Nature of True Faith Matthew 8:5–13 A centurion's servant	17
3. Restored and Strengthened Matthew 8:14–17 Peter's mother-in-law	21
4. Something Ordinary into Something Special Matthew 14:13–21 Feeding a large crowd	27
5. God of the Impossible Matthew 14:22–36 Walking on the water	31
6. Authority over Evil Matthew 15:21–28 The Canaanite woman	35
7. The Power of Faith Matthew 17:14–23 A boy with a demon	39
8. Give to God What Is Due Matthew 17:24–27 The temple tax	45
9. Priorities Mark 2:1–12 A paralyzed man is lowered through the roof	49

Contents *(continued)*

10.	Hearing God's Message and Passing It On Mark 7:31–37 A man who is deaf and mute	55
11.	Spiritual Sight Mark 8:22–26 A blind man at Bethsaida	59
12.	Potential Mark 11:12-25 The withered fig tree	63
13.	Coping with Storms Luke 8:22–25 Calming the storm	67
14.	Authority over Sickness and Death Luke 8:40–56 A dead girl and a sick woman	71
15.	A Loving Response Luke 13:10–17 A woman healed on the Sabbath	75
16.	Thankfulness Luke 17:11–19 Ten men with leprosy	79
17.	Filled with the Holy Spirit John 2:1–11 Water into wine	85
18.	Perseverance in Prayer John 5:1–15 The healing at the pool	91
19.	Life after Death John 20:1–31 Jesus's resurrection	95
20.	Doing Things in God's Strength John 21:1–14 Miraculous catch of fish	99

Appendix: The kingdom is like . . .   103

About the Author

Patrick Coghlan is the pastor of Worstead Baptist Church in Norfolk, England. He has considerable experience working with all age groups, both in the church and in the community. As a Baptist minister, he provides pastoral care and teaching, regularly takes school assemblies, leads services for the elderly in residential care and sheltered housing, and is actively involved with a Christian community care charity.

Patrick is married to June. They have two children: Rachel and Jonathan.

As well as being a Baptist minister, Patrick is a trained Christian counselor and an enthusiastic author. His published books consist of Christian resource material for adults and young people, and several family novels.

Introduction

As you read the Gospels, do you ever wonder why Jesus doesn't heal everyone who is sick, restore sight to all who are blind, enable all those who are deaf to hear, feed everyone who is hungry, etc.? The question still comes up in today's world: Why does God heal some and not others? Some have been hurt by cruel accusations of lack of faith ... but the fact is that sometimes God chooses to heal and sometimes not. I would not presume to explain God's purposes in this respect or to make judgment on the faith or commitment of others. However, I would pick up on John's Gospel (John 3:2 and 20:30) where the miracles of Jesus are referred to as "miraculous signs." Signs of what? Remember the way in which Jesus sometimes introduces his parables by saying, "The kingdom of heaven is like ... " (Matthew 13:24). I believe that in the miracles of Jesus we see glimpses of the kingdom. In other words they are demonstrations of God's power and also illustrations of qualities that will be experienced in the kingdom of God: some here and now, and some when Jesus returns. *The Fragrance of Jesus* is a personal journey through a selection of his miracles, drawing out strands of spiritual significance from them.

The title of each chapter is also its theme. Underneath the title are the Bible references for the miracle on which the chapter is based. Where appropriate, additional quotations—or references—from scripture are used to reinforce the spiritual lessons (taken from the New International Version). Included in bold print are some useful subheadings. Under the heading "The kingdom is like ... " are some questions on which the reader can pause for thought. Each of the questions is preceded with this phrase as a reminder that the purpose of this study is to understand more about the kingdom of which Jesus speaks so much. They are followed with a short phrase highlighting a characteristic of the kingdom. At the end of each chapter there is a prayer of response which may be used as it stands, as a guide, or not at all. It is a good idea for the readers to keep a personal journal, in which they can jot down what they feel God is saying through this journey of discovery, and also any matters for prayer.

The appendix at the end of the book looks briefly at some of the parables about the kingdom. Time and time again we see those involved in Jesus's miracles undergoing a life-changing experience. Indeed, the study of scripture (in this case, miracles and parables) should be a life-changing voyage of adventure.

1. Freedom

Matthew 8:1–4   A man with leprosy

What kind of things make us itch? Nettle stings, mosquito bites, gnat bites, wasp stings ... We are told by the experts not to scratch: so what do we long to do? "Just one scratch!" Thereby lies the dilemma of having a plaster cast on some part of our body: when it itches, how do we reach that point of irritation? Now imagine having an incurable skin disease where the irritation is unending and progressive ...

In New Testament times there was no cure for the skin disease of leprosy. And due to the highly contagious nature of some of its forms, people who had it were driven out of their homes and communities, away from their loved ones, to join communes outside the towns and villages—more than likely, never to return. Imagine the fear and suffering they must have endured, and that feeling of rejection as they were ostracized from society.

> ### The Kingdom is like ...
> Do you believe in miracles?
> What are the reasons for your answer?
> ... When God's power is at work
> miracles happen.

When Jesus comes down from the mountainside a man with leprosy approaches and kneels before him, begging to be healed. I visualize the disciples keeping a safe distance ... just in case! What does Jesus do? He reaches his hand out toward the man. It doesn't say so in the Bible, but we can imagine the disciples shouting words of warning: "Be careful: don't get too close . . . " Too late! Jesus gently touches the man, being careful not to hurt him or cause further discomfort. Immediately the man's skin is healed and restored. Jesus sends him to the priest to be proclaimed free from the dreadful leprosy. The man heads off to begin his life anew. The fear has gone. His skin is clean and unblemished. Maybe he leaves with a new determination not to waste any time or opportunities that lie before him, and to grab hold of that special family time he's been missing out on.

> **The Kingdom is like . . .**
> What do you understand by the word freedom?
> . . . A place of freedom.

Set Free from the Hold of Afflictions

The man in the story is cured from his disease and released to live a normal, active life in the context of family, work, and society in general. However, freedom does not always mean being cured from disease, removed from a difficult situation, released from a struggling relationship, or an end to sadness and fear. Sometimes the miracle is one of being set free from the feelings of imprisonment, restriction, and hopelessness that can arise from enduring such things. And so, that freedom is actually the divine enablement to move forward, lead a fulfilled life, and to be the people God intends us to be . . . despite the ongoing affliction.

Spiritual Freedom

Freedom is also about being released from guilt and set free to move forward in our spiritual lives. Linked with this, freedom is about being released from the consequences and the hold of sin. Romans 3:23 tells us that we are all affected by the disease of sin in our lives. In other words, we have all fallen short of God's standards. Humanly speaking, we have no cure for it.

> *For all have sinned and fall short of the glory of God...*

However, Romans 3:24–25a gives the answer to our predicament.

> *...and are justified freely by his grace through the redemption that came by Christ Jesus. God presented him as a sacrifice of atonement, through faith in his blood.*

Justification is all about being forgiven or made to be as if we have never sinned. Redemption refers to the penalty or price for our sin being paid for us by Jesus's sacrifice on the cross. To understand atonement, think about a pair of scales with two pans: they will only balance when the same weight is on both sides. Grace means that we have done nothing to deserve or earn these things. Let's put it simply: Jesus's death on the cross has paid the penalty for our sin. He rose again and is alive today, so through repentance and faith in him we can receive forgiveness and cleansing from our sin. That means an end to all the consequences of sin—in part now, and in full when Jesus returns—and a fresh new start: All expressions of his love for us.

> **The Kingdom is like . . .**
>
> When did you last speak to someone else about your faith?
>
> . . . There is good news to be shared.

Telling Others

The man cured from leprosy is told not to tell anyone. Compare this with Acts 1:8.

> *"But you will receive power when the Holy Spirit comes on you; and you will be my witnesses in Jerusalem, and in all Judea and Samaria, and to the ends of the earth."*

When we have experienced the healing touch of Jesus on our lives, setting us free from sin's consequences, we are called to share our personal experience of Jesus with others: our families, neighbors, friends, work colleagues, and so on. We do not need to do it with our own strength, because we are promised the empowerment of the indwelling Holy Spirit.

Prayer of Response

Lord Jesus,
Thank you that in you, I am able to find freedom.
Set me free from the things that hold me back,
    in order that I might be able to lead a fulfilled
    life, despite afflictions.
Thank you for being prepared to suffer and die
    on the cross for me;
the penalty for my sin has been paid in full.
Thank you for the touch that heals and cleanses me
    from sin, which
    all people can receive through repentance
    and faith in you—The Risen Lord!
Help me to draw near to you
    in repentance and faith for the first time
    (or to renew and refresh my commitment to you).
Speak into the hearts of those who have
    turned their backs on you.
Touch the lives of those who suffer in body
    with your love, peace, and strength.
Grant me courage and wisdom as I seek to share
    my personal experience of you with others.
In your name I pray.
Amen.

2. The Nature of True Faith

Matthew 8:5–13 A centurion's servant

We live in a society where there is great emphasis on the physical, where belief is so often based only on things that are tangible by sight, touch, smell, taste, or hearing. There seems to be the constant desire to be able to prove everything . . . and the things that cannot be proven or defined in physical terms appear to be placed into serious doubt or even denied completely. Surely, it is the fact that God is indefinable, impossible to contain, does the impossible, and offers that which cannot be proven that is part of what makes him God!

> **The Kingdom is like . . .**
>
> Have you ever been in a position of authority over others? If so, what have you learned from the experience? Does it help you to understand the attitude of the centurion and the authority of Jesus?
> . . . Keep looking to the leadership and authority of Jesus.

Maybe you are still in such a position. The centurion in the Bible passage knows what it is like to instruct people to do something, and then leave them to get on with it. And this life experience appears to have given him a tremendous understanding of the authority of Jesus—and the enablement to believe. Jesus offers to go to the place where the valued servant is living, to heal him. The centurion stops Jesus, believing not only that he has the power to heal the man, but also that there is no need for him to physically go to him... a command from a distance is quite sufficient. Jesus is amazed at the centurion's faith.

> **The Kingdom is like ...**
> What is your definition of faith?
> ... Have faith and believe in the promises of God.

Faith and Belief

Remember what it says in Hebrews 11:1

> *Now faith is being sure of what we hope for and certain of what we do not see.*

And also John 20:29

> *Then Jesus told him, "Because you have seen me, you have believed; blessed are those who have not seen and yet have believed."*

Faith means believing without seeing, touching, smelling, hearing, or tasting in a physical sense. The centurion has nothing physical to hold onto to give him proof and assurance that his servant will be healed from a distance—except for the fact that he may have seen some of Jesus's miracles performed in the past or heard rumors about them, and his own experience of authority. Yet in his heart he has the faith to believe that, without going to the sick man, Jesus can still perform the miracle he is asking for. The centurion is happy to go home in the knowledge of Jesus's promise.

The servant is healed at that very moment.

> **The Kingdom is like...**
> What do you associate with the word *promise*?
> ... God's promises will not fail.

This miracle of Jesus highlights the important part that faith and belief play in Christianity, and something of the nature of true faith. Interestingly, the centurion is a gentile (a foreigner), someone who Jesus's followers would least expect to have faith in him. Jesus is surprised that while many of those who have grown up in the established church of the time, and have been taught the scriptures, still refuse to believe, this centurion—presumably unfamiliar with both—demonstrates a wonderful faith, belief, and openness to God's kingdom.

Personal Response

When people realize that I am a Baptist minister they often say things like, "That's interesting, my grandfather was a Methodist local preacher." They seem to say it in such a way as to try and justify themselves by the faith of others. The implication is that being a Christian is something that is inherited through family lines. Of course, that is not the case; neither does it happen through church attendance on its own. It is through repentance and faith in Jesus.

John 14:6

> *Jesus answered, "I am the way and the truth and the life. No one comes to the Father except through me."*

Prayer of Response

God of miracles,
Thank you that you are a powerful and wonderful God.
Help me to learn from the Bible; and grant me the wisdom and strength to apply those things to my daily life.
Grant me the faith to believe the teaching and promises of Scripture concerning your kingdom; even those things that are unseen and cannot be proved by physical means.
Help me not to try to define or contain you within human boundaries, but to wonder at your power and in your creation.
Thank you that, through repentance and faith, Jesus provides the way to be restored in my relationship with you, and to receive all the good things that you have promised.
Help me to approach Jesus in faith and commit (or recommit) my life to him, today.
In Jesus's name.
Amen.

3. Restored and Strengthened

Matthew 8:14–17 Peter's mother-in-law

I know that many people tend to refer to an attack of the common cold as a fluey cold, or even to say "I've got the flu." But in reality, the actual flu can be a serious condition. As with many illnesses, even once the patient has recovered from the illness, a time of convalescence is necessary before restoration takes place.

Peter's mother-in-law is lying in bed with a fever. One would assume it's the kind of illness that would leave her feeling weak and lifeless afterward. But, we are told that when Jesus touches her hand, not only does the fever leave her, but immediately she gets up and begins to prepare lunch for her guests! No signs of weakness or tiredness. Jesus not only heals Peter's mother-in-law, but he also fully strengthens and restores her.

Not only healed but strengthened and restored. Wouldn't it be wonderful to have a pill that would do that when we are infected with some bug or another? It reminds me of the bottles of medicine that we see being sold on some of the old westerns—guaranteed to cure all! But that's fiction.

The Kingdom is like . . .

What do you understand by the word *restoration*?

. . . Jesus offers us forgiveness, restoration and wholeness.

Spiritual Restoration

The miracle that Jesus performs upon Peter's mother-in-law in a physical sense is the same one that he is able to perform in a spiritual sense—one that is offered to the whole of humankind through repentance and faith in him. Jesus not only forgives, he also strengthens and restores.

Forgiveness

In Mark 1:4 we see John the Baptist preparing the way for Jesus's mission to forgive sin.

> *And so John came, baptizing in the desert region and preaching a baptism of repentance for the forgiveness of sins.*

At the Last Supper (Matthew 26:27–28), Jesus highlights that through his death on the cross forgiveness would be available to all.

> *Then he took the cup, gave thanks, and offered it to them, saying, "Drink from it, all of you. This is my blood of the covenant, which is poured out for many for the forgiveness of sins."*

The significance of Jesus's Death and Resurrection

Before his ascension into heaven, the risen Jesus summarizes the significance of his death and resurrection (Luke 24:46–47). In dying on the cross, Jesus paid the penalty for sin. When rising from the dead, Jesus demonstrated that God has the power to overcome even death. The significance is being able to share the good news of the forgiveness of Jesus and the resulting assurance of eternal life—all over the world.

> *He told them, "This is what is written: The Christ will suffer and rise from the dead on the third day, and repentance and forgiveness of sins will be preached in his name to all nations, beginning at Jerusalem."*

The Kingdom is like . . .

The mission of Jesus is to forgive, to strengthen, and to restore. Surely that's worth having . . . and telling others about. What do you think?

. . . Jesus gives us strength in times of weakness.

Responding with Repentance and Faith

Peter highlights in Acts 2:38 that when we approach Jesus in repentance and faith, not only do we receive his forgiveness, but we are also filled with the power of the indwelling Holy Spirit.

> *Peter replied, "Repent and be baptized, every one of you, in the name of Jesus Christ for the forgiveness of your sins. And you will receive the gift of the Holy Spirit."*

Equipped by the Holy Spirit

Ephesians 3:16 (see overleaf) illustrates that it is through the power of the Holy Spirit that we are strengthened and equipped to live out the Christian life of love and witness—the same Holy Spirit who begins that transformation process which will restore the likeness of God within us (Genesis 1:26).

I pray that out of his glorious riches he may strengthen you with power through his Spirit in your inner being.

The Kingdom is like...

God gave us all freedom of choice. Why does God give us the opportunity to say "no" to all the good things he offers to us?

  . . . It's your choice!

Prayer of Response

God of forgiveness,
Thank you that through repentance and faith in Jesus,
   not only do people receive forgiveness, but they are
   strengthened and restored through the power of the
   indwelling Holy Spirit.
Help me to allow the Holy Spirit to work fully in my life:
that he might enable me to let go of the things I do
   that are not according to your will and values;
for his strength and guidance to help me make good use
   of the opportunities you set before me to share the love
   of Jesus with others and to be his witness;
and that I might be restored into the person that you
   would have me be.
In Jesus's name.
Amen.

4. Something Ordinary into Something Special

Matthew 14:13–21 Feeding a large crowd

"There is bound to be somewhere there where I can get some food," I tell myself as I head out of the house, totally unprepared. "A sandwich, burger, or doughnut shop...or at the very least a street vendor who has chips, soda pop, and chocolate bars."

Perhaps you are more organized. I have friends who never seem to leave the house without preparing a travel mug of coffee and a snack—just in case!

That is the basis of this miracle of Jesus. Everyone has come out unprepared. Maybe they didn't expect to listen to Jesus for such a long time. Perhaps they didn't expect to have to follow Jesus quite so far before he stopped to heal people and tell some of his wonderful stories. Did I say "everyone"? Well, there is someone who has brought five bread rolls and a couple of sardines—or something like that! Fat lot of good they will be to feed everyone. Anyway, dusk begins to fall, everyone is hungry, and the nearest shop is probably miles away.

The disciples want to take the easy way out: "Send them away to the nearest town or village to get themselves some food."

Jesus tells his friends, "No need to do that, you can organize a picnic for them!"

Imagine the panic, "That's crazy! How on earth do you expect us to feed all these people? Be reasonable."

> **The Kingdom is like...**
> What would your reaction have been
> to Jesus's instructions?
> Maybe Jesus has already called you to do the "impossible":
> how did you react?
> ... All things are possible with God.

All Things Are Possible with God

But thereby lies the crux of this parable: in earthly terms, with human strength, this is an impossible situation; but not with divine intervention—that's another ball game altogether. Jesus sits everyone down, thanks God, breaks the bread and gives it to the disciples to hand out. He does the same with the fish. Everyone is fed and there is far more left over than Jesus started with.

Something Special

The miracle here is not just feeding a huge crowd with one person's picnic. No; it is all about what happens when Jesus intervenes! A tiny picnic becomes a meal for thousands of people. Something small and insignificant becomes huge. A task that is completely and absolutely impossible—humanly speaking—is completed successfully. Just so when we ask Jesus to be involved in our lives and offer our resources to be used for his kingdom. Exciting and wonderful things begin to happen: our meager talents and abilities are blessed and multiply, our insignificant lives suddenly play a part in God's huge eternal plan for creation, and those impossible tasks that God calls us to do become possible in the power of the Holy Spirit.

4. SOMETHING ORDINARY INTO SOMETHING SPECIAL

> **The Kingdom is like . . .**
> How has your life changed since following Jesus in faith?
> If you haven't yet done that, then how
> would you like your life to change?
> . . . Thinking about others: generosity and sharing.

Sharing

The starting point of the feeding of the crowd is the generosity of the person who allows the five loaves and two fish to be used in this way. When God is at work, our small demonstrations of generosity can have a tremendous and widespread effect on others.

> **The Kingdom is like . . .**
> Are you prepared to offer all that you have and are to Jesus to use in his service?
> What would that entail?
> . . . Equipped by God.

It's God's World!

The parable about talents in Matthew 25:14–30 speaks about the way in which God entrusts us with a variety of resources; and with that comes the responsibility to use them well. They are such things as the talents and abilities God has given us, spiritual gifts, time, possessions, money. Remember what happens to the man who fails to use his resources—he loses them. Think about the story of the widow's coins in Mark 12:41–44. She gives all that she has to live on to be used for God.

When we are prepared to give everything to Jesus—our whole lives and all our resources—he can do the most wonderful things with them.

Prayer of Response

Lord Jesus,
Thank you that you can take something ordinary and
   seemingly insignificant and do amazing things with it.
Thank you that you can do the same thing with my life.
Grant me a sense of the responsibility that comes with the
   gifts, abilities, and other resources that you have given
   me.
Make me generous.
Take all that I am and all that I have, to be used in your
   service.
Help me to make a significant difference for you,
   in the world today.
Enable others in the world to come to that point of
   realizing that they too need to have you in their lives.
Fill me anew with your Holy Spirit.
Amen.

5. God of the Impossible

Matthew 14:22–36 Walking on the water

Human experience tells us that certain things are impossible—and that includes walking on water. Therefore, it is not surprising that the disciples are frightened at the sight of a figure in the distance, walking toward them, doing just that. However, we are told in Mark 10:27 that nothing is impossible for God.

> *Jesus looked at them and said, "With man this is impossible, but not with God; all things are possible with God."*

The Kingdom is like . . .
What is your response to Mark 10:27?
. . . God is in control.

Try to imagine the situation: the light isn't good, it's hard work rowing against the oncoming waves, everyone is tired after a long day, when suddenly they spot a shadowy figure approaching them on the surface of the water. The disciples' immediate reaction is that it must be a ghost.

Jesus sensing their fear shouts out to them with words to the effect of "It's OK, it's only me!"

Peter, impulsive as ever, is eager to walk out to Jesus. Following his call, Peter leaps out of the boat and to everyone's surprise begins to walk on the water. Suddenly his focus moves from Jesus to the waves around him. Panic sets in, and he begins to sink. His focus changes once again as he cries out to Jesus for help. Jesus reaches out and leads Peter to the safety of the boat.

Keep Focused on Jesus

There are times in our lives when human experience tells us that there is no way through a particular difficult situation. The way ahead seems impossible... Maybe at those times we are guilty of allowing our focus to leave Jesus and rest on the waves around us; in other words, the enormity of the problem and multitude of its negative aspects. We flounder around, trying to cope in our own strength and with our own devices. But Jesus is close at hand, and will help us to deal with these situations when we call out to him in faith—through prayer.

> **The Kingdom is like...**
> What is your understanding of faith?
> ... No need for proof: faith is enough.

A Step of Faith

> *Now faith is being sure of what we hope for and certain of what we do not see.*
> Hebrews 11:1

Sometimes we are called to step out in faith like Peter: to move out of our comfort zone or to perform some task that maybe we feel inadequate to do. It could involve something like changing our job, moving to a new house, or taking on extra responsibilities; or it could be sharing our Christian faith with, for example, a neighbor, friend, or family member. If Jesus calls us to take a step of faith, we can be assured that he will be with us all the way—ready to reach out to us and uphold us when we cry out to him.

> ### The Kingdom is like . . .
> What difficult situations would you
> like Jesus to help you with?
> Is Jesus calling you to step out in faith?
> What is he asking you to do and what is your response?
> . . . Jesus guides, protects, provides,
> strengthens, and helps.

Prayer of Response

Lord Jesus,
Son of God,
Thank you that you are able to do the impossible!
Thank you that through following you in faith,
    you are close by me all the time:
    in the good times, and in times of difficulty.
Thank you that when I cry out in faith, you are there
    to uphold me and lead me to a place of safety.
Help me to remain focused on you at all times;
    and not to become distracted by negative things
    or endeavor to do things with my own strength.
Give me courage at those times when you ask me
    to step out in faith, so that I might complete the tasks
    that you put before me.
In your name I pray.
Amen.

6. Authority over Evil

Matthew 15:21–28 The Canaanite woman

It is important not to underestimate either the power or the busyness of the devil in the world. He appears in the guise of a serpent in the third chapter of Genesis, trapping Adam and Eve with his lies and deceit, starting with those familiar words:

> *"Did God really say . . . ?"*
> *Genesis 3:1b*

Later on, in the book of Job, the devil (Satan) appears before God with the angels. Job's horrendous suffering is a result of Satan's intervention. It is interesting to note that not only is Satan answerable to God, but his power of evil is limited by God.

> *The Lord said to Satan, "Very well, then, everything he has is in your hands, but on the man himself do not lay a finger."*
> *Job 1:12a*

Still at Work

The devil is still at work in so many different ways in the world today. He sows lies, deceit, doubt, and confusion as he strives to destroy God's plans for the good of creation. The devil comes in many different disguises; he even wears badges that give a degree of credibility on occasions; but his intentions are always destructive. He can appear in the form of peer pressure, advertising, marketing, ambition . . . and if he can find a foothold in the Church, he will! The effects are not just spiritual. In practical terms such things as the splitting up of families and communities, materialism, addictions, crime, and immorality are all the fruit of the devil at work in modern society.

The devil even appears to Jesus in the wilderness in Matthew 4:1–11, trying to shape the forthcoming ministry of Jesus to suit his own purposes. Needless to say Jesus refuses to be part of Satan's work; he looks to God's word for the answers to the devil's taunts.

> *Jesus answered, "It is written..."*
> *Matthew 4:4a*

The Kingdom is like . . .
What can we learn from Jesus's response to the devil?
. . . There is no place for the devil.

Power over Evil

The story about the Canaanite woman is a story about faith, about God's power over evil, and it also highlights that the kingdom is for people from all nations of the world. It is the woman's faith that leads her to approach Jesus, and to persist despite him challenging her about her nationality. It is the woman's faith that leads to her request being granted.

The daughter is set free from demonic possession. While living in a world that has been damaged by sin and in which the devil is hard at work, we so need the guidance of Scripture, the example of Jesus, the power of the Holy Spirit, and God's protection upon our lives, through faith and prayer. Look at Ephesians 6:10-20.

> *They will make war against the Lamb, but the Lamb will overcome them because he is Lord of lords and King of kings—and with him will be his called, chosen, and faithful followers.*
> Revelation 17:14

> ### The Kingdom is like . . .
> Think about Revelation 17:14. It's all about Jesus winning the final victory over the powers of evil; and his followers sharing in that victory. Using your imagination, what do you think that will be like?
> . . . Jesus is victorious over evil.

A Witnessing People

In the Old Testament, the Israelites are called to be a witnessing nation. And though in the Gospels Jesus's ministry is primarily aimed at the Jews, the intention is still that they should be a witnessing nation. It's a lovely cameo portrayed in this miracle of Jesus. Yes, the food intended for the children shouldn't be thrown to the dogs; but there will be unwanted scraps that the dogs will devour eagerly. The kingdom was always intended to be for all nations—and it still is! It is big enough for everyone!

Prayer of Response

Jesus:
Lord of lords and King of kings,
Thank you that through your death and resurrection the final victory over sin and evil will be yours; and that as long as I follow you with repentance and in faith I will share in that victory with you.
Grant me your protection against evil and help me, when I am tempted to do wrong, to look toward the Bible.
Empower me through your Holy Spirit to turn away from that which is not pleasing to God.
Thank you that the kingdom is available to all people who follow you in faith.
Strengthen my faith I pray.
Amen.

7. The Power of Faith
Matthew 17:14–23 A boy with a demon

When did you last move a mountain? Having lived in Norfolk, England, for virtually all of my life so far, I am used to people commenting on how flat the county is. True, we do not have any particularly high hills, and certainly no mountains. Although we do seem to have more than our fair share of mole hills! But in this instance, I don't think Jesus is referring to physical mountains ... more those enormous and immovable situations that we face from time to time in life's journey.

> **The Kingdom is like ...**
> Are you facing any mountains at the moment that need dealing with?
> What are they?
> ... Faith can move mountains.

Faith with Expectation

The man in the story takes his son to Jesus's disciples to be set free from demonic possession—but they are unsuccessful in carrying out his request. And so his next attempt is Jesus himself. Jesus proceeds to cast the demon out. Interestingly, he doesn't go to the disciples and reprimand them; it is they who come to him asking:

> *"Why couldn't we drive it out?"*
> Matthew 17:19b

Jesus's reply is that they lack sufficient faith and expectation. I know that at times I have prayed for things that God has laid on my heart to pray about, but with the attitude: nothing is going to change. It is easily done; especially when we may have lived with a situation for many years. I'm sure we can all associate with the disciples' feeling of failure: those missed opportunities, because of lack of faith, expectation, courage, or commitment! So often, when those occasions are viewed retrospectively, we realize what we should have done and what we could have said.

> ### The Kingdom is like . . .
> Have you lost faith or do you feel that you are no longer moving forward in your Christian life because of past failure? Have you prayed for faith and to be released from the bondage of failure?
> What effect has that had on your situation?
> . . . A fresh start.

A little Faith Goes a Long Way!

Jesus gently emphasizes how important faith is when being involved with building the kingdom . . . "As small as a mustard seed," are Jesus's words in the middle of Matthew 17:20. The point is that things don't come much smaller than a mustard seed. What Jesus is saying is that the amount of faith necessary is achievable; even taking into account the depth of human weakness. The miracle is God's; the power is God's; but our faith is the key to unlock that power.

Strength, Courage, Peace, and Determination

Though not appropriate in the case of demonic possession, in some cases the miracle isn't the taking away of the situation, but the ability to deal with it . . . and come through it, often stronger for the experience.

We are not told what the thorn in the flesh is, which Paul talks about in 2 Corinthians 12:8–9, but it appears to be something debilitating that he constantly battles with.

Three times I pleaded with the Lord to take it away from me. But he said to me, "My grace is sufficient for you, for my power is made perfect in weakness."

Indeed many people today struggle, as they have to live with things like disability, disease, and the effects of old age. But look at all that Paul achieves in his ministry—despite the thorn in the flesh with which he battles!

In such cases, the part that faith plays is in accepting that the situation isn't going to change significantly or go away, in the knowledge that through it, God is working his purposes out in some way, and that he will provide the strength, courage, peace, and determination to come through. It is important to remember that God doesn't instigate suffering, but he can use it for good (Romans 8:28).

The Kingdom is like . . .

Have you prayed repeatedly for yourself or a loved one to be set free from a "thorn in the flesh"—and feel that God is saying "no"?

Why do you think that is?

Have you tried praying that God's will be done?

. . . Acceptance of God's will.

God's Will Be Done

> *He went away a second time and prayed, "My Father, if it is not possible for this cup to be taken away unless I drink it, may your will be done."*
> Matthew 26:42

Jesus knows he faces inevitable death as he prays in the garden of Gethsemane before his crucifixion. He pleads with God that there might be a way out; but comes to that point of acceptance that God's will must be done—even if it means dying on the cross.

Prayer of Response

Almighty God,
You are the God of miracles.
Thank you that you are powerful.
Thank you that you love me and care for me in whatever
    situation I am in.
I bring to you my worries and concerns: for myself
    and others . . .
[in silent prayer mention names and situations].
My desire is to be set free from those difficult situations;
    but your will might be to demonstrate your power
    in enabling me to endure them for a purpose.
Grant me faith.
Give me strength, courage, peace, and determination.
In Jesus's name.
Amen.

8. Give to God What Is Due

Matthew 17:24–27 The temple tax

I always admire anyone with administrative abilities; in particular those who are able to do bookkeeping—especially if they can reconcile the balances. A job that I dread each year is preparing the necessary information for my tax return form. But, I have to admit, then I hand everything to the accountant. We do live in a country where life in general seems to involve so much filling in of forms, keeping records, and being accountable to the authorities. As a Christian, I often wish I could be free from paperwork, in order to really focus on doing the work of Jesus here on earth as he commands us to (Acts 1:8). The dilemma is that, as followers of Jesus, though our focus is on the things of God's kingdom, our feet are securely placed in the physical world.

> **The Kingdom is like...**
> How do you think we should approach living on earth, and yet still remain focused on God and his kingdom?
> ... Setting an example to society.

Dual Citizenship

In Matthew 17:24–27, Peter is caught up in a similar dilemma, facing the issue of paying temple tax. Jesus performs a miracle and provides the money to pay the tax. Later on, in Matthew 22:15–17, Jesus is questioned about paying tax in a more general sense:

> *Then the Pharisees went out and laid plans to trap him [Jesus] in his words. They sent their disciples to him along with the Herodians. "Teacher," they said, "we know you are a man of integrity and that you teach the way of God in accordance with the truth. You aren't swayed by men, because you pay no attention to who they are. Tell us then, what is your opinion? Is it right to pay taxes to Caesar or not?"*

After examining a coin, with the head of Caesar on one side, Jesus comes to his conclusions (Matthew 22:21b):

> *"Give to Caesar what is Caesar's, and to God what is God's."*

Indeed when we have committed our lives to Jesus in faith, we effectively have dual citizenship. We are members of God's kingdom but, at the same time, we are also part of earthly society. As such, we have responsibilities to God, but also we have responsibilities to pay toward the earthly services that are provided for us to enjoy and benefit from. As an aside, we also have an obligation to be obedient to the laws of the land—as long as they do not compromise God's values. If they do, then we need to lobby government to change them!

The Kingdom is like . . .

Are there areas of the law of the land that you feel compromise God's values?
If so, what are they and how do you think they should be changed?
. . . No compromise.

Give to God What Is God's

What does it mean to give to God what is God's? Genesis 1:27 tells us that God created us in his own image—with the aim of sharing fellowship with us. 1 John 4:19 tells us that God loved us first. John 3:16 talks about God allowing his Son, Jesus, to give his life on the cross for us, paying the penalty for our sin—as a demonstration of that love. 2 Corinthians 5:17 speaks about God recreating us through faith in Jesus. God has given so much. Apart from our thanks, what should we give to God?

> **The Kingdom is like...**
> How could you give more of yourself and your resources to God in service?
>   ... Give ourselves to God as an act of worship.

> *Therefore, I urge you, brothers, in view of God's mercy, to offer your bodies as living sacrifices, holy and pleasing to God—this is your spiritual act of worship.*
> Romans 12:1

Paul calls for us to give ourselves to God as an act of worship: all that we are, all that we can be with God's help, all that we say, and all that we do. That calls for selfless commitment and focus. "Give to God what is God's."

Prayer of Response

Loving and generous Father in heaven,
You have given me so much!
You created me in your image, to share fellowship with
    you, Jesus, and the Holy Spirit.
In your love, you provide for me, guide me, and have
    made it possible for me to be forgiven and recreated,
    through faith in Jesus.
Thereby lies my eternal hope!
I thank you and praise you ... and offer myself in worship.
Transform me, through your Holy Spirit, so that I might
    be more like Jesus himself; empower me,
      to serve you in building the kingdom;
      and be strength in my weakness.
In Jesus's name.
Amen.

9. Priorities

Mark 2:1–12 A paralyzed man is lowered through the roof

I am sure that we are all familiar with having the odd tile lifted from our roof, especially in older properties. It may even have resulted in that telltale dripping of water through the ceiling below. I understand that is not unheard of for burglars to break in by removing tiles from the roof and cutting through the ceiling. But I am sure that you wouldn't expect passing visitors to drop in through the roof just to see how you are, would you?

News has spread about the wonderful miracles and parables of Jesus. People gather from far and wide, turning up at Capernaum. They squeeze into the house where Jesus is, line up at the door, and lean in at the windows. Jesus is hemmed in from all directions. Meanwhile a group of men are making their way to the house, carrying a friend who is paralyzed. When they arrive, they are confronted with, what might seem to be, an insurmountable situation. Many would have given up at far less. Perhaps the paralyzed man utters words like, "Thanks anyway...you gave it your best shot but it just wasn't meant to be." But the men who had carried him there are focused on what they have come for and do not intend to go home until that has been achieved. They demonstrate strong qualities such as determination, persistence, ingenuity, imagination, boldness, courage, and resourcefulness. They get themselves and their friend onto the roof and begin to hack their way through. We can imagine the crowd looking up at the ceiling in bewilderment, and hastily moving to one side when they begin to realize what is happening.

Suddenly a hole appears and a head pops through, "Watch out, below, a man is coming down." Maybe ropes are available or possibly the men improvise ropes with clothing. Soon the man is lying on his mattress, in front of Jesus, in the clearing. "Hi Jesus, my friends brought me." As the man's eyes indicate the whereabouts of the men, a selection of faces look down from above. "Hi lads: are you OK up there?" They nod together, grinning like the cat that has got the cream ... and Jesus can see their faith and depth of friendship for the man they have brought.

Imagine their surprise when Jesus tells the paralyzed man, "Your sins are forgiven." Never mind what the teachers of the law are thinking; what about the men who have managed to get their friend in to see Jesus, despite the extreme difficulties?

> ## The Kingdom is like . . .
> How do the priorities in your
> life match up with the teaching of Jesus?
> . . . God first.

Correct Priorities

Primarily, this miracle is concerned with correct priorities. In practical terms, life is so pressured and busy that we need to prioritize. Sometimes the obvious choices aren't the most helpful ones—or the most appropriate to God's values. The things that we think we need are not always what we actually need. Sometimes these and other areas are gray, and we need discernment from God. For example, in a materialistic world, often the *desire* for more unnecessary wealth and possessions override our intrinsic *need* for rest and to spend quality time with our families and God.

> *"Remember the Sabbath day by keeping it holy. Six days you shall labor and do all your work, but the seventh day is a Sabbath to the Lord your God..."*
> *Exodus 20:8–10a*

Vanity and selfishness can stand in the way of caring for others. The priority that Jesus sets in this miracle is that spiritual healing is more important than physical healing—gained through repentance and faith in him. Indeed, it has eternal consequences. Not to belittle the reality of human suffering and how to deal with it; or the importance of how we live in the *here* and *now* ...

> ### The Kingdom is like ...
> Think about a world where friendship, caring for others, and spreading the love of Jesus is more of a priority in people's lives. What effect do you think it would have on modern society?
> ... Built on love.

The Value of Friendship, Caring, and Love

This is also a story about commitment, friendship, caring for others, and Christ-like love in action. Sadly, commitment seems to be quite a rare thing these days, in our impulsive, self-centred, throwaway society. The friends are not content until the errand of mercy has been completed. Thank God for friends like that and such a level of commitment. Their love could so easily have been in word only; but Christ-like love expresses itself in selfless actions as well.

> ### The Kingdom is like . . .
> What are your strong positive qualities and how have they helped you to overcome difficult times and serve Jesus effectively?
>   . . . One body with many parts;
>   each with positive qualities.

Positive Qualities Are Needed

What amazing positive qualities we see demonstrated by the friends—determination, persistence, ingenuity, imagination, boldness, courage, and resourcefulness. These qualities are so necessary in life—tools to help us cope with adversity; together, of course, with strength and enablement from God. Where would we be without such qualities as we strive to do the work of Jesus here and now—being the body of Christ? (1 Corinthians 12:12–31)

Prayer of Response

Almighty God,
Thank you that through Jesus you have brought hope and spiritual healing to a damaged world.
Thank you for the power of the Holy Spirit to guide, transform, and strengthen me.
Thank you for love and friendship.
Thank you that in your wisdom you have equipped me with positive qualities to help me deal with difficult situations and to serve you more effectively.
Help me to make the correct choices as I prioritize day by day and as I prepare for eternity.
Enable me to be a loyal friend and to actively demonstrate your love to others.
Help me to remain positive in situations that can lead to despair.
In Jesus's name.
Amen.

10. Hearing God's Message and Passing It On

Mark 7:31–37 A man who is deaf and mute

When it comes to gossip, some of us seem to be very good at hearing and passing on—even when there is doubt as to the truth of its content. The things we hear about others are often not ours to pass on: it is like stealing what doesn't belong to us. What is it about gossip that makes it so attractive? In general, there is not quite the same enthusiasm to pass on the truth of the Christian message to others, even though we have been commissioned to do so. Also, again in a general sense, people in the twenty-first-century world are more reluctant to listen to the life-changing message of Jesus, than to scandal.

Mark 7:31–37 is the account of another amazing miracle of Jesus. Not only is the man's hearing restored, but immediately he is equipped and able to speak fluently.

> **The Kingdom is like . . .**
> Where do you look to for your source of help and strength during difficult times? Why?
> . . . Help in a crisis.

Coping Day by Day

At one level, this is a story about disabilities—physical and mental. There is a wide variety of disabilities that people have to cope with in the world. Some pass with time or surgery, others are life long. This miracle involves a man who has to cope with deafness and not being able to speak fluently. Maybe there are additional problems linked with this, like being ostracized from society, struggling to earn a living because of discrimination, perhaps there are feelings of rejection. We are told that the man has been brought by a group of people—perhaps they are friends, members of the family or maybe caregivers. They beg Jesus to heal him. Though in this particular case the man is cured, in reality there will be times when, no matter how much praying in faith goes on, a person will not be cured of his or her mental or physical illness or disability. The prayer then becomes one of desiring to experience things like acceptance from others, to be given the strength to cope day by day, to receive God's guidance, to become more adaptable, and that God will provide people who care.

As with so many areas of human suffering, hardship, and endurance, God's miracle isn't the removal of the source, but the enablement to rise above the situation in different ways, and still lead a fulfilled life.

> **The Kingdom is like . . .**
> Could you share your testimony with others?
> What would you say?
> . . . It's for sharing.

Equipped to Witness (Acts 1:8)

The spiritual parallel of this account of healing is that, through prayer and a close relationship with Jesus, the Holy Spirit will grant us the ability to hear what God is saying to us through Scripture—and other ways—and pass it on. To put it another way, we will be able to move beyond the words and understand the deeper spiritual truths contained (see Luke 8:10), and will be given the ability to share those truths—and our personal experience of Jesus—with others. The boldness, courage, opportunities, and words to speak will be provided.

Prayer of Response

Loving Lord Jesus,
Thank you for the good news to be shared with others
 about you.
Give me the courage and confidence to share with others
 something of my own story:
to talk about my relationship with you,
and what it means to follow you.
Thank you for the Bible;
give me a real hunger to learn more about you
 from Scripture, and help me to pass it on.
Through the power of the Holy Spirit help me to be
 a faithful follower of you.
Be with those who suffer from disabilities:
let them be treated with care and dignity;
enable them to rise above those things that seem to be
 restricting them;
grant them the opportunity to fulfill the dreams that you
 have set before them.
In Jesus's name.
Amen.

11. Spiritual Sight

Mark 8:22–26 A blind man at Bethsaida

Remember that well-known question: Is the glass half full, or half empty? It is a good illustration of the dilemma of so many of life's situations: Do we take the positive viewpoint, or the negative?

There is an excitement as the half-finished house is visited by the purchasers. "Look how far they have got!" one might exclaim excitedly. "But there is still so much to be done. We'll be lucky to be in by Christmas," another adds.

In the Bible passage, the man's sight is restored in two stages. At first he is able to see the outline of people *"like trees."* I wonder what he is feeling as he looks around at the onlookers and they appear only as faint images. It doesn't say in the account, but maybe he had lost his sight in later life, knowing what it was like to be able to see clearly. Perhaps he feels disappointment that the result of Jesus's touch has fallen short of his expectations. But then a second touch completes the job and he is able to see clearly.

Jesus doesn't make a mistake, or lack the power . . . In performing this miracle, in the way he does, Jesus is demonstrating yet more characteristics of the kingdom: the first is patience and the second is the progressive nature of God's revelation.

> **The Kingdom is like . . .**
> In what areas of your life could you demonstrate more patience?
> How could you do it?
> . . . Be patient.

Patience

Patience is not something that comes easily to us living in today's "instant" society. Everywhere we look the symptoms of impatience appear, for example, road rage, folks getting into huge amounts of debt, mistreatment of elderly people. Learning to be patient, without becoming apathetic or complacent, is a valuable lesson.

Patience in the Kingdom

These are just a few examples of passages in the Bible that refer to patience being very important in the kingdom.

Romans 12:12 highlights the need for patience in affliction:

> *Be joyful in hope, patient in affliction, faithful in prayer.*

1 Corinthians 13:4a highlights the need for patience in love:

> *Love is patient.*

Galatians 5:22 places patience as one of the fruit of the Spirit:

> *But the fruit of the Spirit is love, joy, peace, patience, kindness, goodness, faithfulness . . .*

James 5:7a highlights the need to wait patiently for the second coming of Jesus:

> *Be patient, then, brothers, until the Lord's coming.*

Revelation 14:12 calls for patient endurance:

> *This calls for patient endurance on the part of the saints who obey God's commandments and remain faithful to Jesus.*

We should remember that God's timing is perfect—it is worth waiting for!

> **The Kingdom is like . . .**
> What do you understand about the term *spiritual maturity?*
> Think about the significance of things like prayer, Bible study, and church membership to our relationship with Jesus. How do these reflect on your journey with Christ?
> . . . God wants to reveal his purposes.

Progressive Nature of God's Revelation

This miracle highlights that, in a spiritual context, God reveals his purposes progressively. Equally so, the understanding of Scripture and its application revealed by the Holy Spirit is linked in with spiritual maturity—an ongoing process that relies on our walk with Jesus.

Prayer of Response

Gracious God,
Thank you for your faithfulness and promise to
　　humankind.
Thank you that your timing is perfect.
Grant me patience in all my dealings with others,
　　especially those who are vulnerable.
Help me not to become complacent or apathetic.
Strengthen me and others in adversity—
　　and give me patience.
Help me to demonstrate patient endurance as I await
　　the return of Jesus.
Be with those who are vulnerable, for example,
　　children and young people, the elderly, those who are sick
　　or suffer from some kind of disability.
Protect them from the impatience of others.
Surround them with your peace and love.
In Jesus's name.
Amen.

12. Potential

Mark 11:12–25 The withered fig tree

Living in the country for most of my life, I have become accustomed to hearing people come out with a variety of sayings relating to things like the weather, gardening, and farming. I wouldn't like to say which are true and which are not, but there are definitely certain future happenings that can be predicted with some accuracy simply by using common sense, experience, and knowledge. There is much that the sky can tell us about imminent weather conditions. I am sure that animals, with their acute senses, can indicate bad weather on its way. To a trained eye, even during the winter months, the examination of a cutting or two will soon reveal if a deciduous tree or bush is still alive. Equally so, the lack of blossom on an apple tree indicates a lack of fruit later in the season.

Potential

Though Jesus's action concerning the fig tree appears harsh, as it is not the season for fruit anyway, in reality his judgment is based on the absence of any signs that would indicate potential fruitfulness. Jesus knows that as the leaves of the tree are out in full, there should be signs of the little tiny immature figs appearing—the potential for a harvest later in the season.

> **The Kingdom is like . . .**
> A sack of grain will feed a family for a limited time, but what is its potential if the seed is planted?
> Are there ways in which your potential to produce spiritual fruit could be increased?
> . . . God-given potential.

The parable about the talents (Matthew 25:14–30) is concerned with God-given potential. It is saying that we have all been entrusted with a variety of talents and abilities that can be used in the kingdom—and in a deeper sense this includes other resources that we are responsible for. Whether or not we choose to use them is up to us. Those who make good use of talents and abilities for God will find that they develop and bring even more blessing to others. Some, sadly, either misuse their talents, abilities, and other resources in a self-centered way, or fail to make any use of them at all. The tragedy highlighted in the parable is that of wasted resources. Indeed, ours is a very wasteful society.

It is so important to nurture the potential of young people, and those who have become discouraged and broken by circumstances. Also, we need to respect the potential for wisdom of older people, gained from knowledge and life experience.

> **The Kingdom is like . . .**
> What talents and abilities has God given you?
> What are you doing with them?
> . . . Full of opportunity.

Lack of Fruitfulness

The purpose of a fruit tree is to bear fruit.

In John 15:1–8 Jesus talks about the vine and the branches. . . . In this parable he emphasizes not only that we need to have a close walk with him through faith, but also that our purpose is to produce spiritual fruit (Galatians 5:22–23a).

12. POTENTIAL

> *But the fruit of the Spirit is love, joy, peace, patience, kindness, goodness, faithfulness, gentleness, and self-control.*

Those who don't will be dealt with harshly.

Prayer of Response

Generous heavenly Father,
Thank you that you have given everyone talents
  and abilities to be used in your service,
  to help build your kingdom.
I thank you for the talents and abilities that you have
  given me.
Help me to use them for you, to benefit others.
As I use them, and endeavor to build them up through
  training and practice, develop them and refine them.
Help me to be an encourager of others,
  especially those who have been broken by life's
  experiences.
Fill me anew with the Holy Spirit,
  and also your love to share with others,
  in so doing enable me to be fruitful.
Help me personally, and society as a whole, not to waste
  the valuable resources that you provide...
or damage—for future generations—
the world in which we live.
In Jesus's name.
Amen.

13. Coping with Storms

Luke 8:22–25 Calming the storm

I have fond memories of exploring the Norfolk Broads, a series of rivers and lakes, as a young man in a rowing boat and on my Dad's smallmotorboat. There was always a wonderful peacefulness during the winter months, when most of the holiday boats were moored up. I recall quite strong tides in places, the odd shower and blustery wind ... but never a fearsome storm. Maybe you are a person who loves boats, and have had the unfortunate experience of being caught in a fierce and maybe life-threatening storm. Apparently the Sea of Galilee is renowned for its violent storms.

As we look at this miracle, it is important to remember that a number of Jesus's disciples are experienced fishermen. They are not unfamiliar with the ways of the Sea of Galilee. So the severity of this particular storm must be something out of the ordinary; such that these men genuinely fear for their lives. Jesus remarks on their lack of faith as they wake him up to deal with the situation. Imagine their relief as he stands up and calms the wind, the rain, and the raging waves.

> ### The Kingdom is like . . .
> Bearing in mind Genesis 1:1-31 it is not surprising that Jesus has authority over the natural order of things.
> What do you think and why?
> . . . God is the Creator.

Safe with Jesus

The crux of the story is that despite the ferocity of the storm, with Jesus in the boat, they are in fact safe all the time. But I am sure that we can still emphathize with the disciples' fears. Sadly fear is not a good listener to logic and reason—or truth. In a broken world the battle against things like fear tends to be an ongoing one, about which we need to be constantly in prayer.

When we commit our lives to Jesus in faith he will be with us as we face those difficult, fearful, and stressful situations that we come up against in life: bereavement, sickness, loneliness, difficult decisions, disappointments, problems with relationships, debt, unemployment, and so on. He might not make the situation go away, as in the case of this miracle; but he will equip us to deal with the immediate situation and we can be sure that, from an eternal perspective, he will keep us safe! Thereby lies our hope.

> **The Kingdom is like . . .**
> Are you facing a metaphorical storm
> in your life at the moment?
> If so, what is it?
> How does it make you feel?
> What are you going to do about it?
> . . . Jesus is listening.

Only a Prayer Away

It is a comfort to know that Jesus is only a prayer away: waiting for us to reach out to him in faith. Having lived on earth, he knows what it is like to undergo things like hardship, suffering, and sadness. He is interested in our lives and longs to share in both the good times and the difficult ones. He is with us always when we follow him in faith.

> *"And surely I am with you always, to the very end of the age."*
> Matthew 28:20b

Burdens Made Light

And he longs to make our heavy burdens light.

> *"Come to me, all you who are weary and burdened, and I will give you rest. Take my yoke upon you and learn from me, for I am gentle and humble in heart, and you will find rest for your souls. For my yoke is easy and my burden is light."*
> Matthew 11:28–30

Prayer of Response

Lord Jesus,
Thank you for your love and promise that, when anyone
    has faith in you, you will always be with them.
Thank you that you are concerned about the difficult and
    fearful situations that I face [take time to name them]:
    and long to relieve something of the burden that
    I bear.
Thank you that you understand what it is like to suffer
    and go through different human feelings and emotions.
Please strengthen my faith; help me to prayerfully allow
    you to share the burden that I bear.
Empower and guide me through the storms of life.
Thank you for the eternal hope of safety that I have in you.
Be with others who suffer and are anxious; and help them
    in their time of need.
Amen.

14. Authority over Sickness and Death

Luke 8:40–56 A dead girl and a sick woman

Are you a lover of crowds: concerts, the theater, carnivals, mass transit...? I recall an occasion at Oxford Circus when my family and I were hurrying along when all of a sudden we met a vast crowd: no one was moving in front and soon people began pressing in from behind as well. I began to feel quite claustrophobic, and at the same time, fearful for my children's safety. Whatever could cause such a build-up of people? Before long, a helicopter could be heard approaching; it landed in the middle of the wide road, obviously to pick up a casualty of sickness or accident—quite a feat of flying!

> ### The Kingdom is like . . .
> In the story, what do the lady's actions say about Jesus's touch?
> . . . The touch of Jesus brings comfort, peace, healing, and hope.

The Healing Touch

Wherever Jesus goes, a crowd seems to follow him. The passage above is no exception. When Jesus returns, large numbers of people await. As Jairus speaks to Jesus about his dying daughter, a sick woman approaches Jesus and touches his clothes, in faith and expectation. She is cured instantly from a twelve-year affliction. Then Jesus astounds his disciples by asking, "Who touched me?" How could he say such a thing when people are pushing and shoving from all directions? But Jesus is aware that power has gone out from him; and the miraculous has happened. Jesus goes on to raise Jairus's daughter from death, even after the servants tell Jairus not to bother the teacher any more as it is too late!

Two stories linked together. Both stories demonstrate the effect of receiving the touch of Jesus during difficult times, and what it means to include Jesus in all our life situations. We live in a world that is broken by the effects of sin: our own sin, the sin of others, and the inherent effects of sin past. As we struggle to cope with the ongoing symptoms of a sin-damaged world, we can experience tremendous comfort, peace, and hope as we experience Jesus' touch upon our lives.

> ### The Kingdom is like . . .
> What part do things like prayer, Bible study, and fellowship have in encouraging spiritual health and strength?
>
> . . . Jesus' touch is healing.

Spiritual Health

There is an ongoing spiritual healing as we walk with Jesus in faith. And as we involve Jesus in our daily lives, we begin to experience the hope of eternal life in his presence.

No More Suffering and Death

But, from this passage of Scripture, we can also learn that when we experience God's kingdom in all its fullness (when Jesus returns) there will be no more sickness or death. Indeed, the glimpses we get from this and other stories about the miraculous healing powers of God and his ability to raise the dead reinforce the fact that in the kingdom there will be no more sickness or death—as the power of God is greater even than those things.

Prayer of Response

Lord Jesus,
Thank you that, when anyone reaches out to you in faith
 and expectation, wonderful things happen.
Grant me that kind of faith.
Thank you, that when people involve you in their lives,
 they begin to experience the hope of eternal life,
 in your presence—
and receive your peace and comfort.
Help me to walk with you.
Thank you that in the fullness of your kingdom there is
 no more sickness or death.
Be with those who are sick at this time;
 and those suffering bereavement.
In your name I pray.
Amen.

15. A Loving Response

Luke 13:10–17 A woman healed on the Sabbath

> *"Remember the Sabbath day by keeping it holy. Six days you shall labor and do all your work, but the seventh day is a Sabbath to the Lord your God. On it you shall not do any work, neither you, nor your son or daughter, nor your manservant or maidservant, nor your animals, nor the alien within your gates. For in six days the Lord made the heavens and the earth, the sea, and all that is in them, but he rested on the seventh day. Therefore the Lord blessed the Sabbath day and made it holy."*
> Exodus 20:8–11

There is not much that people won't consider doing on a Sunday these days: stores are open, leisure facilities function as normal, all manner of sport takes place, and huge numbers of people are expected to work. I recall hearing my parents' and grandparents' generations talking about the days when even the potatoes would be harvested from the garden and peeled on a Saturday, so as not to have to work in preparing them on a Sunday. Our society has slipped from one extreme to the other. I believe that neither extreme reflects God's intentions for us.

An Expression of God's Love

We see a similar extreme in the society into which Jesus is born. The miracle in this passage takes place on the Sabbath day. Thereby appears to be the crux of the passage. Jesus has healed the woman. The problem is not *what* he has healed and restored her of but the fact of *when* the act has been performed. The man in charge of the meeting place confronts the people about the issue (Luke 13:14b).

> *"There are six days for work. So come and be healed on those days, not on the Sabbath."*

The Kingdom is like . . .
How can we fulfill the fourth commandment, without falling into the same trap as Jesus's opposition?
. . . Ruled and guided by God's love.

Jesus points out the hypocrisy of such legalism that allows people to care for their animals on the Sabbath but not for each other. He uses the analogy of someone being set free from being bound up. The law of God is an expression of his love. It is for the good of his people. Nothing in God's law can be detrimental to us, or the purposes of his kingdom. Unfortunately, through the generations, governing bodies have not always held onto that principle; and the law has become distorted and in ways harmful to society.

The Kingdom is like . . .
What does the world of advertising have to say about love?
. . . Jesus' death on the cross is an expression of his love for us all.

The mission of Jesus is about releasing people from the entrapment of sin and its consequences. The death of Jesus on the cross is yet another expression of love.

> *This is how we know what love is: Jesus Christ laid down his life for us.*
>   1 John 3:16a

Contrast this with the message that our modern western society seems to be promoting—that of satisfying self-centered desires.

> **The Kingdom is like . . .**
> What is your response to the risen Jesus?
>   . . . It really is your choice!

Varying Responses

Finally the passage highlights the divided responses to the things that Jesus is doing. Indeed the response to Jesus will be varied. Some will recognize Jesus as God's Son, believe his message, and respond with repentance and in faith. Some sadly will fail to recognize God at work and will make no positive response to Jesus's call.

Prayer of Response

Loving heavenly Father,
Thank you for all your expressions of love showered
 upon your creation; including the giving of your
 commandments.
Help me to understand and obey them.
Thank you that Jesus died on the cross so that everyone
 might have the opportunity to be set free
 from the entrapment of sin and its consequences—
 and that he rose again.
Let my response to him be one of repentance and faith.
I pray for the world today: that people might look to you
 for their values, strength, joy, hope, and freedom.
In Jesus's name.
Amen.

16. Thankfulness

Luke 17:11–19 Ten men with leprosy

As a child, it was always instilled into me to say please and thank you. I think maybe other people of my generation would say the same about their own experience. It annoys me intensely when I go into a shop and, not only do the staff carry on a conversation with each other while serving, but they also fail to remember those small words: please and thank you. The miracle recorded in this passage focuses on our response to answers to prayer and the provision of God more generally.

> **The Kingdom is like . . .**
>
> Have there been times in your life when God's answers to your prayers have been "no" or "wait" . . . or maybe, though the answers have been in the affirmative, they have taken forms that were contrary to your hopes and expectations?
>
> Were you still able to give thanks to him?
>
> . . . God guides and provides in many different ways; for which we should give thanks.

God's Provision and Answers to Prayer

Word has obviously got around concerning Jesus's power to heal. A group of people suffering from the terrible skin disease of leprosy are waiting for him as he approaches the village. They are outcasts from society because of the contagious nature of their illness. Being aware of the restrictions that bind them, they shout out to Jesus from a distance (Luke 17:13): "Have pity on us!" The men's call to Jesus is one of faith and expectation. They believe that what they are asking is possible, and that it will happen. Oh for such faith and expectation in our prayer lives ... but their healing is not instant—they are called to wait.

In a way, Jesus gives the ten men a challenge, asking them to take a step of faith first—before their request is answered (verse 14): "Go, show yourselves to the priests." At this stage the men are not healed because, later on in the same verse, it says: "And as they went, they were cleansed." Faith plays a large part in the kingdom. Indeed, there are times when we are called to take that step of faith: as it were, to take the first step in response to God's calling, trusting that he will be faithful in honoring his promises. A good illustration of this is Peter's literal step of faith as he endeavors to walk out on the water to Jesus (Matthew 14:22–33). Following the call of Jesus, Peter steps out of the boat knowing that in human terms what he is attempting is completely impossible. After achieving the first few steps, doubt crowds in on him and he begins to sink, but Jesus is there to hold him up above the waves.

Sometimes a lack of thankfulness can be caused by not recognizing God's provision to us or the answers to our prayers; or simply not accepting the answers he gives, for example, when he says, no—for our own good; wait—for his perfect timing; or fulfills our prayers in a way that is different from our hopes and expectations.

The Kingdom is like . . .

Have you become part of God's wonderful heavenly family yet? It is open to everyone.
Do you remember to give thanks to Jesus for providing the way (John 14:6)?
. . . God is the perfect parent to have—be thankful.

Transformed Lives

The ten lepers *tick all the boxes*. They have reached out to Jesus in faith and with expectation; they have taken the required step of faith; and awaited God's perfect timing. As a result, the miracle has happened. Their greatest wish has been granted: to be made well, to be able to enter into society again, and to be restored in their relationships with their families. In Psalm 91:15a it says, "He will call upon me, and I will answer him." Just as physical healing leads to the ten men being reunited with their families, so the prayer of repentance, commitment, and faith in Jesus leads to spiritual healing, restoration in our relationship with God, and entry into his heavenly family. New Testament teaching on judgment indicates that there will come a time when a selection will take place on the basis of that relationship.

The ten lepers have so much to say thank you for . . . but do they? When we enter into God's heavenly family, how much more should we be giving thanks?

> *Is not the cup of thanksgiving for which we give thanks a participation in the blood of Christ? And is not the bread that we break a participation in the body of Christ?*
> 1 Corinthians 10:16

> ## The Kingdom is like . . .
> How much of your prayer is demands and how much is thanksgiving?
> ...We have a lot to thank God for.

Saying Thank You

There is a double surprise in this miracle. Firstly, despite the fact that all ten have been healed, only one of them returns to say thank you to Jesus. Sometimes, we have so much that we just take things for granted. At times we just become so focused on other things that saying thank you to God is forgotten. There is a lack of thankfulness in this miracle; and more generally in the world today.

Also demonstrated in this healing of the ten men with leprosy is that God's provision in many ways is enjoyed by all, even those who don't follow him and are not thankful to him—such is the extent of God's love. There is a need for more thankfulness to God.

> *Give thanks to the Lord, for he is good; his love endures for ever.*
> 1 Chronicles 16:34

16. THANKFULNESS

You turned my wailing into dancing; you removed my sackcloth and clothed me with joy, that my heart may sing to you and not be silent. O Lord my God, I will give you thanks forever.
Psalm 30:11–12

Prayer of Response

Almighty God,
Thank you that you are powerful, just, faithful, and
 loving.
Thank you that, through Jesus's death and resurrection,
 the way has been opened up for all people to be healed
 spiritually and to enter into your eternal heavenly family.
Thank you that you answer prayers offered in faith
 and expectation.
Help me to recognize those answers and your provision;
and to be willing to accept your will and perfect timing.
Help me to be more thankful.
I thank you for… [name examples]
In Jesus's name I pray.
Amen.

17. Filled with the Holy Spirit

John 2:1–11 Water into wine

We've probably all been to functions where either the food or drink has run out. It is embarrassing joining the food line, and all that is left is half a plate of sandwiches, a sausage on a stick, and a few chips. Do you sit in a corner and pretend not to be hungry, take a single sandwich and try to make it last, or point out the dilemma to the host? I have to admit that I would probably go for the first option.

Try to imagine that moment of realization at the wedding in Cana: "There is no more wine left. What shall we do?" It was a little indiscreet of the servants to allow it to be known to the guests, perhaps! I love that mother–son moment as Mary turns to Jesus with the expectation that he will put things right—maybe not expecting a miracle, just a bit of practical advice. Jesus's reply is a little difficult to understand. Maybe he is indicating that this is not really the right place or time for a miracle ... but, despite Mary probably not fully understanding the reply, she knows that she can safely leave it in Jesus's hands to do what is best in the situation.

The six stone water containers are there for ceremonial washing—a reminder of the legalistic misinterpretation of the law in operation. This miracle involves a change of use—new things! Traditionally, the word *change* has tended to cause people in the Church to be on their guard: "We've always done things this way!" Admittedly, change for the sake of change and change in respect to compromising God's standards is not good, but moving with the times, keeping up with God's leading, and keeping a freshness about the way we function in the Church has to be good.

> **The Kingdom is like . . .**
> How do you feel about change?
> . . . It involves new things.

Jesus's Ministry Is Associated with Change

> *When Jesus had finished saying these things, the crowds were amazed at his teaching, because he taught as one who had authority, and not as their teachers of the law.*
> Matthew 7:28–29

These verses highlight that Jesus's teaching comes as something new from that of the established Church—with "authority." Not only is Jesus's teaching new, but he also heralds a new way of doing things in God's plan for salvation (being set free from the consequences of sin). No longer does the old sacrificial system, involving animals, apply—Jesus's death on the cross marks the sacrifice that need never be repeated. But his ministry also involves leading people away from the misinterpretation of the laws of God by the established Church. In Matthew 5:17–20 Jesus makes a point of saying that he has not come to abolish the law, but to help people understand the true application of it. The law of God is an expression of his love for the benefit of humankind!

> **The Kingdom is like . . .**
> Have a look at the Ten Commandments (Exodus 20:1–17). How is God's love reflected in them?
> . . . All the commandments are for the good of humankind.

A Law Based on Love

The six stone water containers find a new use at the wedding in Cana. No longer are they used for ritualistic cleansing, but they become part of a joyful and fulfilling celebration of two people in love with each other coming together in marriage. The law of God should not be a ball and chain: laws with no purpose for the sake of laws. The coming of Jesus marks an end to legalism. His teaching and example to us is based on things like love, forgiveness, compassion, fellowship ... and ultimately a bringing together of the Church and himself when the kingdom comes in all its fullness. This is described in terms of the bride and groom coming together at the wedding (for example Matthew 25:1–13, the parable of the ten virgins).

> **The Kingdom is like ...**
> The Church is people who have committed to Jesus in repentance and faith—being empowered and transformed by the Holy Spirit. What is your response to that?
> ... All its members progressively transformed more into the likeness of Jesus himself.

Transformed by the Holy Spirit

The miracle of water into wine demonstrates quite a transformation. When we commit our lives to Jesus in repentance and faith, we are filled with the Holy Spirit who begins an ongoing transformation within us.

> *And we, who with unveiled faces all reflect the Lord's glory, are being transformed into his likeness with ever-increasing glory, which comes from the Lord, who is the Spirit.*
> 2 Corinthians 3:18

That transformation will be made complete when Jesus returns.

> *But we know that when he appears, we shall be like him, for we shall see him as he is.*
> 1 John 3:2b

> ### The Kingdom is like . . .
> Life with Jesus is the best.
> What are you going to do about it?
>   . . . It is the best!

Life with Jesus Is the Best!

There is surprise at the wedding feast that the best wine has been saved until the end. It is no surprise that the wine Jesus supplies is the best. Indeed life with Jesus is the best—it doesn't get any better! And yet sadly so many people keep putting off making that commitment to him. Why put off something as good as that, which could be enjoyed right now? And when you have made that commitment, don't keep it to yourself.

Prayer of Response

God who loves to give good gifts,
Thank you for the gift of the indwelling Holy Spirit.
Fill me anew.
And help me to be willing to allow him the freedom
    to transform me into the person you would have me be.
Thank you for the teaching of Jesus.
Help me to be willing to accept change when it is
    according to your will.
Thank you that life following Jesus in faith is the best!
Help those who are still searching for meaning, purpose,
    and fulfillment in life to meet personally with him.
In his name I pray.
Amen.

18. Perseverance in Prayer

John 5:1–15 The healing at the pool

It is surprising what we can get used to and learn to live with. When I broke my leg, initially the full-length plaster cast almost immobilized me. When I broke my leg a second time, a few months later, I found by that time I was an expert at travelling over a variety of terrains and obstacles with my crutches. Indeed we can become used to dealing with and accepting all kinds of different adverse circumstances: in a negative way, we stop complaining, learn to live with it, and come to the conclusion that nothing is going to change.

It was believed that the pool of Bethesda had miraculous healing qualities; such that the first person in the water after it had moved in a particular way would be healed.

Feelings of Hopelessness

Jesus asks the man in the story if he wants to be healed. Why? It probably seems to be a silly question to us. However, the invalid's reply confirms Jesus's theory. After thirty-eight years of hoping for a cure and of struggling to reach the water at the appropriate time, he has become tired of trying, filled with the hopelessness of the situation, and accepted that things aren't going to get any better. Imagine his surprise when Jesus tells him to get up and walk.

> ### The Kingdom is like . . .
> How does it feel when God seems to be saying either "no" or "wait" in reply to your prayers? Maybe God is testing your faith, or the timing is not right. What does this mean?
> . . . God will answer your prayers and he knows best.

Keep Praying

Sometimes the people or situations that we have been praying for, maybe for many years with no apparent result, leave us feeling that nothing will change. It could be that God is saying "no," or if God has really laid it on our hearts to keep praying about that person or situation, then he is probably saying "wait" until the time is right. When we pray, we need to do it with faith and expectation—believing that God can do and still does the miraculous.

> **The Kingdom is like . . .**
> Why do we sometimes fail to recognize God's answers to our prayers?
> . . . God is working his purposes out.

Watch out for God's Answers

Some, if not all, of the onlookers are sidetracked by the misinterpretation of God's laws that they have been brought up with. They are so concerned about the rights and wrongs of carrying a rolled up mattress on the Sabbath that they fail to see the amazing miracle that has taken place. Indeed, sometimes we can get distracted—maybe with thoughts of how we believe God should be answering our prayers—so that we fail to see how he is actually answering them. We must keep alert, so that we don't miss seeing God's hand at work.

> **The Kingdom is like . . .**
> God opens up windows of opportunity: why do we sometimes fail to make use of them?
> . . . Full of opportunity.

Make Good Use of New Opportunities

The way in which Jesus seeks out the healed man in the temple is interesting. He instructs him to "stop sinning." Jesus seems to be saying, "Make good use of the new opportunities that have been set before you now." One of life's greatest challenges must be to not waste those windows of opportunity that God opens up for us.

Prayer of Response

Lord Jesus Christ,
You are the source of eternal hope.
Help me during times when I am feeling down.
Give me the perseverance to keep praying for those people
   and situations you have laid on my heart,
     even when nothing seems to be happening.
Help me to be sensitive to your answers to prayer,
   even when they are not what I expect.
Grant me the drive and courage to make good use of
   new opportunities.
Uplift those who have been crushed by difficulties,
   and face resulting feelings of hopelessness.
In Jesus's name.
Amen.

19. Life after Death

John 20:1–31 Jesus's resurrection

Living in a sinful world, I tend to be a bit skeptical about some things, like believing that there aren't many occasions when we can receive something for nothing. As I watch certain TV shows I sometimes wonder how spontaneous some of these productions really are. I guess it is part of human nature to be skeptical, especially looking back upon some life experiences. As God performs the amazing miracle of bringing Jesus back to life, he is only too aware of the doubting audience he is working with. Read the Gospel accounts of the death and resurrection of Jesus. There is no doubt that Jesus really died. From the multitude of witnesses to the risen Jesus, before his ascension into heaven, to my skeptical mind the Resurrection is proven beyond any doubt.

> **The Kingdom is like . . .**
> How do you fit into the ongoing story of Jesus?
> . . . It's relevant to your past, your present, and your eternal future.

Help for Today

If Jesus's death had been the end, though we could have still remembered him and learned some useful life applications from his teaching and example, it would probably have been the end of the story. The living Jesus means that the story goes on. The fact that Jesus wants us to relate to him in faith means that the ongoing story can include each one of us. It means that, as we face difficult situations, fear, guilt, shame, sadness . . . Jesus can share with us in those times, strengthen and uphold us through the power of the indwelling Holy Spirit—equally so, we can be empowered as we endeavor to live out the Christian life of love and witness.

Fulfillment of Promise

The birth, life, death, and resurrection of Jesus also fulfill Old Testament prophecy—or you could call it promise from God. It all goes toward emphasizing the point that God is faithful, and his promises never fail!

> **The Kingdom is like . . .**
> Why do we need hope?
> . . . Hope in a world that sometimes appears to be hopeless.

Hope for Eternity

The more we experience the effects of sin on the world in which we live and the resulting hardship, suffering, sadness, and injustice, the more we need the eternal hope that is promised through the resurrection of Jesus. Through repentance and faith in him, we have the eternal hope of a place where those things come to an end (Isaiah 25:6–8). Just as, through our relationship with Jesus, he shares in our present situations, he will also be an intrinsic part of our eternal future.

19. LIFE AFTER DEATH

Prayer of Response

Living Lord Jesus,
Thank you that you are my help for today
 and my eternal hope.
Thank you for the promise in Scripture that,
 when you return,
your followers will be able to enter fully into
 your presence ...
and at that time there will be no more injustice,
 sorrow, or suffering.
Help me to follow your example.
Fill me with your love to share with others.
Grant me the courage to tell others about you.
Amen.

20. Doing Things in God's Strength

John 21:1–14 Miraculous catch of fish

There is a well-known saying, "What are friends for?" It is part of human nature to strive to be independent; but the reality is that we were not created to be so. We were created by God to be interdependent: in other words to relate and work together, with each other and with God. The parable of the growing seed (Mark 4:26–29) illustrates clearly that, in order to be successful, we need to include God in all that we do as we seek to serve him—as we endeavor to fulfill our calling to be part of the body of Christ. In a metaphorical sense, we can prepare the ground, plant the seed, water, and weed … but growth is only possible through the hand of God.

> **The Kingdom is like …**
> Are there times in your life when you have struggled to cope in your own strength, rather than turning to God? If you could go back, would you do things differently now?
> … No longer single-handed.

With God's Help, the Fishermen Can

In John 21:1–14, the fishermen have fished all night and caught nothing! Jesus intervenes, preparing to work a miracle. What the seven disciples are unable to achieve in their strength, is achieved in the power of God through Jesus—a catch of fish so large that the net has to be dragged behind the boat to the shore. How much more this is true in a spiritual sense! Remember Jesus's words to Peter and Andrew in Matthew 4:19, *"I will make you fishers of men."*

With God's Help Peter Can at Pentecost

Following the miracle recorded in John 21:1–14, we see Peter reinstated after denying Jesus following his arrest (John 18:15–18, 25–27 and 21:15–17). Having let Jesus down, we see the Spirit fill Peter, preaching in God's strength at Pentecost (Acts 2:1–47). The result of including God in his ministry, through the power of the Holy Spirit, is that over three thousand believe and are baptized on this one particular occasion.

> ### The Kingdom is like . . .
> On a scale of 1–10 how good are you at depending on God? (10 is very good)
> In what areas of your life could you be better?
> How do you think you could improve?
> . . . You can depend on God the Father, Jesus the Son, and the Holy Spirit.

Learning to Depend on God

A key feature of the analogy of Jesus's followers being part of the "body of Christ" (1 Corinthians 12:12–31) is that there has to be cooperation and interdependence. The body parts need to work together with efficiency—but also be dependent on the head (Jesus himself). As followers of Jesus, we need to learn to depend on the Triune God (God the Father, Jesus the Son, and the Holy Spirit) for guidance, empowerment, and strength on a daily basis in order to live out the Christian life of love and witness. That includes the big things, but also the smaller day-to-day issues involving things like relationships, honesty, work ethics, and decision making.

Prayer of Response

Loving Heavenly Father,
Thank you that you created me to be interdependent:
    give me the humility to allow others to help,
    enable me to put myself to one side and allow you to
    guide, empower, and strengthen me.
Fill me anew with the Holy Spirit.
Give me the desire to learn more about Jesus and to follow
    his example, guidance, and teaching.
Thank you that though, in my own strength, I can achieve
    little as I seek to be part of building your kingdom,
    when I include you, great things can happen.
Grant me the desire to include you in all that I do.
In Jesus's name.
Amen.

Appendix

The kingdom is like...

Matthew 13:24–30 and 13:36–43

> *"The kingdom of heaven is like a man who sowed good seed in his field. But while everyone was sleeping, his enemy came and sowed weeds among the wheat, and went away."*
> Matthew 13:24b–25

Jesus compares the kingdom with a man who plants a field of wheat. But someone else comes along at night and sows weeds among the good seed. As the seeds germinate the dilemma is spotted. The owner of the land decides that the best thing to do is wait until the harvest to separate the good crop from the weeds. This parable describes the eternal nature of the kingdom, emphasizing that judgment is a reality and that there will be a harvest!

This parable reminds us of Genesis 3:1–24 and the book of Job. All three illustrate the eternal picture of God's kingdom, and highlight the point that it is the devil that intervenes and spoils. However, just as Job eventually returns to a point of blessing, so in Genesis 3:15 we read the promise that Jesus will come and rectify the damage caused by sin and evil. In the eternal picture of Creation, initially we see its wonder and perfection. The devil intervenes with the intention of spoiling what God has created and is doing through that creation. He sows lies, doubts, and deceit; playing on human desires and weaknesses. But through Jesus dying on the cross, paying the penalty for sin, rising again, and conquering death, the whole picture changes.

Through him the way is opened up to be restored and re-created through repentance and faith (John 14:6). The victory over sin and evil has been won; and when Jesus returns, his followers will share in that victory—in all its fullness—for eternity (Revelation 17:14).

Two of the many stories that confirm the reality of judgment are the stories of Noah (Genesis 5:1–9:29), and the Tower of Babel (Genesis 11:1-9). Love and justice are two aspects of God's character. Just as he cannot be unloving . . . he cannot be unjust—it is against his nature. But in his love he has made it possible for all to be saved from the consequences of that judgment, through repentance and faith in Jesus.

And that leads us on to the harvest (see Matthew 13:1–23). The impact of the parable of the sower, when Jesus originally spoke it to the crowd, would have been that despite the wasted seed there would still be a harvest! Indeed in Matthew 13:24–30, despite the attempted sabotage . . . there will still be a harvest! There will be those who commit their lives to following Jesus, despite the distractions to turn away from the things of God.

You and I have the opportunity to make a difference to the outcome in the here and now. Ezekiel 3:17 and 33:6 talks about watchmen: people who would keep a look out, and warn of the enemy's approach. As followers of Jesus, we have a responsibility to share the Christian message with others, through word and deed. In so doing, we can help lead others to meet with Jesus for themselves; so that they might experience his forgiveness and recreation through the power of the indwelling Holy Spirit.

Matthew 13:31–33

> *"The kingdom of heaven is like a mustard seed, which a man took and planted in his field. Though it is the smallest of all your seeds, yet when it grows, it is the largest of garden plants and becomes a tree."*
>
> *Matthew 13:31b-32a*

Jesus continues to talk about seeds. He likens the kingdom to the tiny mustard seed, which, under favorable conditions, can grow to the size of a small tree ... such that the birds are able to perch in its branches and find rest. The nature of the kingdom is that from small beginnings, it will grow into something huge—beyond anything that we can imagine. Within it, people will find rest: in terms of spiritual healing, peace, fulfillment, and wholeness. The picture implies that there is an openness regarding entry into the kingdom—through repentance and faith in Jesus, all are welcome.

> *"Come to me* [Jesus said], *all you who are weary and burdened, and I will give you rest."*
>
> *Matthew 11:28*

> *Now we who have believed enter that rest.*
>
> *Hebrews 4:3a*

Those who have made bread, or have watched it being prepared, will be familiar with the qualities of yeast. Its effect is experienced by the whole batch of dough. In this parable (13:33), Jesus once again portrays the extent that the kingdom will grow; but also the way in which it grows. It could well be an illustration of the Holy Spirit at work within followers of Jesus and the world at large. Through faith in

Jesus, a process of transformation begins within us, as the indwelling Holy Spirit progressively transforms us more into the likeness of Jesus himself.

> *And we, who with unveiled faces all reflect the Lord's glory, are being transformed into his likeness with ever-increasing glory, which comes from the Lord, who is the Spirit.*
> 2 Corinthians 3:18

> *But we know that when he [Jesus] appears, we shall be like him, for we shall see him as he is.*
> 1 John 3:2b

Through Spirit-filled individuals, striving to be the people God wants them to be, and the Holy Spirit preparing others to receive and respond to the message of Jesus, communities are changed for the better. The effect escalates, travelling worldwide and across the generations.

Matthew 13:44

> *"The kingdom of heaven is like treasure hidden in a field. When a man found it, he hid it again, and then in his joy went and sold all that he had and bought that field."*

I wonder if you have ever wanted something so badly that you have had a really good clear-out—and sold a variety of things that were no longer in regular use—in order to buy that special thing. In these two parables Jesus paints a picture of this happening. First of all, a treasure hunter makes a discovery in a nearby field. Such is his desire to possess that treasure he hides it again, until he is able to sell all his possessions so that he can buy the field and own the treasure. Next he tells of a dealer in fine pearls, who sells all that he has in order to buy a pearl of outstanding quality and beauty. Such is the kingdom of God.

The point Jesus is making is that nothing can compare with the kingdom in terms of fulfillment, joy, peace, and blessing or overall value. Material possessions are transient. They are destroyed by corrosion, wear and tear, and parasites. We cannot take them with us when we die. The world in which we live at the moment is tainted by the consequences of sin, for example pain, suffering, physical death, fear, guilt. God's kingdom is eternal; we can experience its wonder in part now, but in all its fullness when Jesus returns. Isaiah 25:6–8 portrays the qualities of the kingdom in terms of a great feast.

> *The Sovereign Lord will wipe away the tears from all faces.*
> Isaiah 25:8b

There can be nothing more important or worthwhile in life than seeking and entering into God's kingdom through repentance and faith in Jesus . . . and sharing the knowledge and experience of it with others. Belonging to God's wonderful, eternal kingdom is the most valuable treasure that any of us can ever possess!

Luke 15:1–7

> *"I tell you that in the same way **there will be more rejoicing in heaven** over one sinner who repents than over ninety-nine righteous persons who do not need to repent."*
>
> *Luke 15:7*

In the twenty-first century we might be forgiven for feeling depersonalized: that we are just numbers in a computer. Bills have customer numbers, account numbers, and invoice numbers. Drivers licences, passports, insurance certificates all have numbers to identify us. We even have a patient number at the doctor's.

The parable of the Good Shepherd highlights that in God's kingdom everyone is an individual: unique and special—the shepherd refuses to rest until the one missing sheep is found and returned to a place of safety. The shepherd's care for the sheep represents Jesus's sacrificial love for each one of us. How great is the love of Jesus for us all:

> *This is how we know what love is: Jesus Christ laid down his life for us.*
> *1 John 3:16a*

> *Greater love has no one than this, that he lay down his life for his friends.*
> *John 15:13*

Jesus died on the cross, paying the penalty for our sin, and rose again so that, through repentance and faith in him, we might be forgiven and have eternal hope. That is what we remember and celebrate when we take bread and wine in the communion service.

What a wonderful picture to finish with as Jesus speaks about an amazing party in heaven. There will be celebrations when each individual turns to Jesus in faith and enters into the kingdom. How good is that!